T0007829

I THINK WE'RE ALONE NOW

'In Abigail Parry's second collection, every aperture is haunted. These poems limn the spaces between vertigo and hyperextension, drawing then rethreading the needle through sites of forgetfulness and failure: are you unsure you heard that right? Listen again, Parry's speakers exhort, scraping tines into the grooves of torch songs, scattering speculums and stereotaxic rats into the pages. What the poet pursues, and enacts through a formally blistering surgery of poetics, is nothing less than the upward ruination of the everyday: nothing exists that cannot be unspooled, unknotted, blasted open, wired shut. The body of this work promises blood, and brutality, and ridiculousness, plus every mistake anyone has ever made fletched through with gold. Run into its pages with every weapon you possess. None of them will be enough to keep you unmarked for good.' – SHIVANEE RAMLOCHAN

Abigail Parry spent several years as a toymaker before completing a PhD on wordplay. Her poems have been set to music, translated into Spanish, Serbian and Japanese, and performed or exhibited in Europe, the Caribbean and the US. She has won a number of prizes and awards for her work, including the Ballymaloe Prize and an Eric Gregory Award.

Her first collection, *Jinx* (Bloodaxe Books, 2018), dealt in trickery, gameplay, masks and costume, and was described as 'a party in a bag' (Declan Ryan) and 'vaudevillian sleaze' (Stephanie Sy-Quia). The book was shortlisted for the Forward Prize for Best First Collection and the Seamus Heaney Prize for Best First Collection, and named a Book of the Year in *The New Statesman* (Marina Warner), *The Telegraph* (Tristram Fane Saunders) and *Morning Star* (Kate Wakeling). Her second collection, *I Think We're Alone Now* (Bloodaxe Books, 2023), was shortlisted for the T.S. Eliot Prize 2023.

Abigail Parry

I THINK WE'RE ALONE NOW

BLOODAXE BOOKS

Copyright © Abigail Parry

ISBN: 978 1 78037 681 3

First published 2023 by
Bloodaxe Books Ltd,
Eastburn,
South Park,
Hexham,
Northumberland NE46 1BS

www.bloodaxebooks.com
For further information about Bloodaxe titles
please visit our website and join our mailing list
or write to the above address for a catalogue.

Supported using public funding by
**ARTS COUNCIL
ENGLAND**

LEGAL NOTICE

All rights reserved. No part of this book may be
reproduced, stored in a retrieval system, or
transmitted in any form, or by any means, electronic,
mechanical, photocopying, recording or otherwise,
without prior written permission from Bloodaxe Books Ltd.

Requests to publish work from this book
must be sent to Bloodaxe Books Ltd.

Abigail Parry has asserted her right under
Section 77 of the Copyright, Designs and Patents Act 1988
to be identified as the author of this work.

Digital reprint of the 2023 Bloodaxe Books edition.

For if the watcher of the watcher shown
There in the distant glass, should be watched too,
Who can be master, free of others; who
Can look around and say he is alone?

THOM GUNN, 'The Corridor'

ACKNOWLEDGEMENTS

My thanks to the editors of the following journals, in which some of these poems first appeared: *Poetry London*, *The Moth*, *Interim*, *Southword*, *Poetry Bus* and *Gravy*. Also to the Wellcome Collection, who commissioned 'A beetle in a box', and to Frantic Assembly, who asked me to write about intimacy in the first place.

My love and gratitude to the many friends who lent me their eyes, ears, and wisdom, and in particular to Ailbhe Darcy, Maura Dooley, Tristram Fane Saunders, Holly Hopkins, Ali Lewis, and Shivanee Ramlochan. To Neil Astley, most patient of editors. And to Tristan Hughes, for ignoring all sage advice about poets.

CONTENTS

The brain of the rat in stereotaxic space

is all laid out on numbered plates.
In lilacs, greys and greens, which adumbrate
the local function;
                    a riddle
flattened out. A knot
                    bisected down the interaural line.

The brain of the rat in stereotaxic space
admits no trace
of all the little rat-thoughts, little rat-needs,
that scurry round its maze. Just page on numbered page
of *isthmuses* and *commissures*, and *junctions* and *rhombomeres*,
                                        all jigsawed into place.

The brain of the rat in stereotaxic space
insists the pieces tessellate
and nothing else squeaks in. Just *fig* on numbered *fig*,
                                glossed in 8-point lowercase.

The brain of the rat in stereotaxic space
invites us to extrapolate
and come up with grim stuff –

here's no ghost, no guest, no hidden ace
tucked up a sleeve. No sleeve, in fact. Just stacks of coloured plates.

The brain of the rat in stereotaxic space
has something to relate
about how late it is. How much has been a waste.

Grateful, nonetheless,
to have had my time at a kink of neural space
that more or less exactly corresponds
to that where you had yours –
                    a riddle
uttered once, between one blank page and the next. And that will do, I think.

Speculum

I like the word – how pert it is.
Inquisitive. Part instrument, part
clockwork bird – the kind that says *ho hum*

and clicks and squeaks in all its joints.
A whimsical professor, beaked
and blinking: *let's take a look then,*

shall we? In the Vulgate, it's a mirror:
videmus nunc per speculum.
Only later on are we *through a glass*

and *darkly*. (An odd phrase, that –
a pane of sullen blue behind each eye.
You don't look *through* a mirror.)

You go not till I set you up a glass
where you may see the inmost part of you.
That's Hamlet to his mother. In a sec,

he'll get all weird about her bed
and stick his sword straight through an arras.
As for me, I find it strange to speak

in one breath of one's conscience
and one's cunt. Hard to know thyself,
when for years the only way was with a mirror,

tilted up. For a long time, I believed
it was an absence: blank negative
the lab could not develop. An ellipsis.

Imagine my surprise, to find the way
extended upwards, backwards, inwards.
All the same, I'm bothered by the rhyme

that finds my centre in its recess.
And yes, I find it tiresome to be
arriving in my body, again and again,

each time we talk of what is *intimate*.
No way back now, to the place
where we first looked in a mirror

and cringed into our borders, turning
inwards. But I want a better metaphor than this
dull fuss of sloven pinks, or a room

partitioned off. Like Alice in the sequel,
slipping through, to find everything she knows
inverted on its axis and nonsensical.

Axonometric

I know you understood that *space* to mean
    your negative: dark bolt of antimatter,
cut to fit; a wounding suit of lights
turned inside out. The ego will not countenance the scene

that won't return its gaze. Let me explain.
    Or let me try.
Increasingly, I think of what we say
as a field of broken signposts, or windblown semaphore,

or just bellowed through a keyhole,
    but it hurts to think that you think of yourself
in punched-out sequins, mattes and deadeye feathers
        and I want to get this straight.

I've thought a lot, just lately,
    about the double life of doors and locks and all
the two-way apparatus of control.
In Spanish, there are different kinds of corner:

the outside one – the one you turn around –
    and the one you sit or slump in,
which by extension means you're out of options.
Rincón – that little nook, stopped and shut.

That isn't right. But if I talk around it,
    we'll get the formal scope of it
  in dashes and ellipses.
You know the trick – just blur the mind a little

and feel around the rooms we've built between us,
  with their door codes and their dress codes,
with their twists on you and me.
    Let's tell the truth in this one. Let's agree

I liked myself, refracted in your eyes.
    As switch and mournival and eel spear,
nine heads in nine glass cabinets,
    or nine lives knotted round a single cat;

a ransacked drawer of costumes and positions,
           and shadowboxing rabbits, games
and parlour tricks and military tactics;
                a stack of hand-me-downs

that don't quite fit. That's more like it.
    And something in the Highways Act
I saw the other day: *a door which opens on a street
           shall be so put as not to open outwards;*

which by extension means it opens *inwards.*
           Yes, you've got it,
says the grownup girl in her sudden
shrunken house, with one arm jammed against the only exit.

In the dream of the cold restaurant

the man with the buttonhole and broad lapels
is folding and refolding a white napkin.
Look, say his hands, at intervals. A swan.
A dancing girl. An intricate scale model
of the Maugham Library on Chancery Lane.
The man adjusts his buttonhole and coughs

as each one fails, precisely, to entertain.
A waitress intervenes, bringing two plates –
fluted, plain, translucent. And quite empty.
Such is the gaunt extravagance of dreams.
That waitress, though. All elbows, wrists
and hips. A strip of exposed skin reveals a scar

on the nub of bone that finishes the spine.
No – not a scar. A burn. A full-blown wet rosette,
just like the one you earned at seventeen
from a fuck on a nylon carpet – a carpet
not unlike this carpet here, lalling its beige
hoops and braids around the table's feet.

Meanwhile, on the mezzanine,
someone lifts a book and reads the line
he left his knee exposed, and dreamed
of travelling on a mail coach by night.
Well quite. When you offer up your plate
it turns, beneath your hands, to a crumpled swan.

The man, of course, has gone.
Such is the glib economy of dreams.
So find a way to bear it, if you can –
the man who folds and folds and cannot please,
the cheap carpet, telling its idiot riddle,
the girl who has not learned to move between

compassion and contempt. But then,
other people's dreams are very dull,
as the waitress knows with all the brutal
certainty of being seventeen. And she's gone too.
She'll pull this city to the ground before
she'll take your plate, let alone your pity.

The Swords

Nine shafts   in steely fluency, between
the headboard and the wall
grey-blue
       like ice or gunships   brute and serious
               a face between cupped hands
and all the saints
polite as china mice up on the shelf.
                               Eight
          silver wicket gates
         the minor byways
that span and fret the dark   a painted heart
      ringed round with thorns
      eight hard-pressed fingers groping up to heaven.
                         Seven
           shining hells, assorted demi-hells   *his eyes*
           are humbler than they used to be
           Seven
keys to the too-tall maze   blue
leaves like folded razorblades   you, trapped inside
      or opening the door, not knowing me
         that hissing water lily, blue
         and blue and liquid orange round its ring.
Six bubbles, in a string.
        Now count them – sugar
necklace, stream or abacus
a line of silver, running
from your mouth up to the ceiling
      that's how you know   which way to swim
that's how you know
              which way is up
              Now count them,
                 count again.   Now swim –

                    Five
fins on the propeller
or any large machine that scythes or pumps or stirs the water.
                    Four
          warrior angels, crumpled round their swords.
                    Three
          twins to my unhinged half
          gone missing from the mirror.
                    Two
          black holes where the eyes should be.

One aircrewman, who lives in the museum
his 'chute all rucked and pooled
                    Stubbed

nose of the submarine

Old Man Pike, who sculls the dark
               and one blunt thought,
               its lead balloon: full
                    stop where the air runs out.

Set piece with mackerel and seal

A little bit of hush please, as we help this
gentleman from his bright doublet. To do it well,
hook one thumb into the mouth and pull
revealing the red ruff. They go so quick like that,
as if something came unfastened or let drop
its stocking and stepped out. A flutter, as of silk,
then all the pewter dulling into blues
and deeper blues and greys and indigos.
And light, which has no business with the dead,
trips off to count its costume jewels instead.

The dark is moving in the deeper dark
below the swell, and sometimes, it raises its head
or the skin-on-skull that passes for a head.
Then he blows his ballast, or just lolls, gross
doyen of this house. Shows who's boss.
And what ignites the burner in his brain
is that old flirt, the glint of sun on scale.
Good, perhaps, to be this. To be nothing
but urge and sate and swell. When all there is
to know of light is winks and promises.

Someone is fishing from the morning rocks
on a telescopic pole. With knots and nylon.
He knows there is this fractious glitterball
turning with the tide, and wants answers
to his stilted little rig of luck and will.
He wants to be all nerve, just one nerve,
running up the carbon fibre, down the line,
to where the lures twitch. To cast the spell
and then fall hopeless under it. Till all he knows
of joy looks like a bar of beaten light.

Trickier, to be this. To have this flair
for theatre. For knots and complications.
To learn, again and again, how the diva
might anyhow just flounce off in her sequins.
Not tonight, perhaps. But one day soon.
Then all the houselights dimming into blues
and deeper blues among the shadowed stalls.
And then just empty rows, and empty seats,
and nothing more and no one moving there
but the lean old usher pulling down the shutters.

MARGINAL GLOSSES

English-speaking learners

are often vexed to learn that there exists
no simple verb to indicate possession.
You do not **own** a thing. A thing is **with you**.
What goes with me are those things which are mine.

The house – for example – is **with you**.
A set of keys – the spare set – is **with me**.[1]

[1] With us – in the spatial sense – although
this is of course a matter of contingency.

Do note that this syntactic switch-around
is typical of very ancient languages
and English-speaking learners will, with practice,

subordinate the subject to the rule;
may even come to understand it better
than the English verb *to have*. Its grasping hand.

English-speaking learners

will find their verbal habits are entangled
with nearby Indo-European roots:
to have and hold; *to occupy*, *control*;
to bind or *fetter*. Also: *to remember*.

The interested (or curious) might ponder
the rascal lexicon that More and Giles
dreamed up to serve the people of Utopia:
a jostled rack of globes and astrolabes

which features, in among its vocables,
ꊢ ꄷ △ ꄷ ꒕ – *those things which are mine* –
and ꒦ ꄷ ꄷ ꆢ ꒒ ꒕ ꆤ – *those things which are better.*

We must understand *Utopia* as satire.
Still, the interested (or curious) might wonder
just how peaceably these two might share an island.

English-speaking learners

may encounter an ingenious sophistry
whereby all thought – each mental irk and imp –
is circumscribed precisely by the terms
of the language that we use to name the urge.[2]

    [2] See *Messrs Sapir, Whorf.* See *Orwell, George.*

Which is to say – the mind is only free
so far as it is sanctioned by the tongue
to which it's tethered. A brute beneath its yoke.

English-speaking learners who would bridle
might remember Lydgate, John:

    Bewar of tungis double and deceyuable.

Note how quickly your own comes to the palette
like a clapper in a bell, for the stroke
of *no* and *not.* For singing *never, never.*

English-speaking learners

will notice, in this version of the Psalter,
that the faithful lift their *twohand*, not their *hands*.
The noun is singular, but names the pair:
clasped together, as it were, as if in prayer

or bound about the wrists. The verb agrees.

In English, too, are several terms that cleave
unto their opposites. As in the verb *to bless*.
As in – we *lift our hands* but *raise our fists*.

Consider, for example, the word *free*.
As in *free from obligation*; *free from care*;
from bondage, subjugation. Do note the irony

by which the word must name its own constraint;
learners would do well to remember
that we never speak of one without the other.

COVERS

I Think We're Alone Now

It's stuck in there, the thought.
>   *Running just as fast as we can*
>   *Holding on to one another's hand*
It's wound up really tight.
>   *Trying to get away   into the night*
Two minutes only to complete
its unicursal not-quite-circuit
>   *And then you put your arms around me*
the loop where you and I play out
those stubborn gestures on repeat –
>   *And we tumble to the ground*
the crickets bleat their string quartet,
the synth does its forever bit
>   *And then you say*

Les jeux

Les jeux

sont faits. Or so he says. The croupier –
Les jeux sont faits. Rien

ne va plus. But wait, what's this,
here's Bogart with a tip –

      perhaps you'll try your luck on 22.

Well well, Monsieur. *Quelle veine.*
Now take your chips and go –

The table's cold, the wheel is stalled,
the house is done with you.

      As honest as the day is long. Quite so.

La partie

continue. Remember when we walked into
that backroom in Macau –

I'd said it all the way, I'd said
RED and 28,

I'd just one bet to make, and it was
RED and 28.

A red note in my pocket,
one red number in my head,

and just one bet to make – all on
RED and 28.

But I dithered between tables
and the wheels wouldn't wait –

      No more bets. Les jeux sont faits –

and the nearest wheel came to rest
                on RED and 28.

Rien

ne va plus. How long ago was that?
Ten years –
              more like fifteen.

And all the while this body
went on kicking out its freight

tick tick tick

      like bloody clockwork.

Your chances of it happening now
are roughly 1 in 20

and me, I'm still not ready.
Not ready, never sure enough, amazed
so many were so ready.

Les jeux, I guess,
sont faits. The chips are down.
No more bets.

Or the one I like the best, the one
that gives it to me straight
on a blunt and simple instrument –

           Too late.

Mesdames, Messieurs, I like a term
that sounds like what it is –

Too late,   Too late,   Too late,

a falling tone, a slowing wheel,
the rattle of the plate

and a little double zero
where it buckles at the waist.

Whatever happened to Rosemarie?

Your song is on the radio again, Rosemarie.
The one where every other line is *Rosemarie, Rosemarie.*
He acts likes he can't hear it, but I see it, Rosemarie –
how the backrooms of his brain have all lit up with ROSEMARIE.
A ten-foot neon sign, and it's flashing ROSEMARIE
in ten-foot neon letters, that go *Rose* and *mar* and *ee.*
And he's turning drunken circles arm-in-arm with Rosemarie
in a seedy little dive bar. And the bar's called *Rosemarie's.*

I found a load of photographs – they're all of Rosemarie –
he keeps them in an album labelled *Me and Rosemarie.*
There's a little punctured heart above the *R* of *Rosemarie*
and it lives beneath the bed you chose together, Rosemarie,
the bed he shares with me. And he mumbles *Rssermuree*
when he's asleep and dreaming all his dreams of Rosemarie.
And I can't quite shake the feeling I'm intruding, Rosemarie,
when the springs inside the mattress squeal *Ro-semarie, Ro-semarie* –

  Ro-semarie, Ro-semarie – *Ro-semarie, Ro-semarie* –

There's a signpost in his heart that points the way to Rosemarie
and beside it there's a suitcase that belonged to Rosemarie
and inside it there's a pocketbook inscribed with ROSEMARIE
with two tickets for the steamer ship, the SS *Rosemarie.*
Yes, the past's a foreign country, and its queen is Rosemarie,
and he worships at the altar of its Venus, Rosemarie.
I can't understand the language – every word is *Rosemarie*
and the picture in my passport couldn't pass for Rosemarie.

Someone sack the archer – he's *obsessed* with Rosemarie
and every dart is loaded with that poison, Rosemarie.
In every corner of my heart, there's a knife for Rosemarie
and they've all got secret nicknames – but the nickname's Rosemarie.
And in this light – and if I squint – he looks a bit like Rosemarie.
Just add a bit of lipstick... yes, like that, like Rosemarie.
Now tell me that you love me. Say your name is Rosemarie
and kiss me like she kisses. Say I'm yours, my Rosemarie.

It is the lark that sings so out of tune

He's up at dawn again. She stays in bed.
She runs through all the stupid things she said
and *almost* said when she got in last night.
Quite late again. Quite drunk – or drunker than
she meant to be. And spoiling for a fight.
Loathèd toad, she thinks. She burrows in
and in the half-light underneath the covers
she thinks half-thoughts and half-remembers others.

Like how much is behind her. How much less
is still ahead. The days that come and go
like dull beads on a joyless abacus.
She listens, as he potters round the kitchen.
She hears him going through the old routine
she knows by heart: the cheery, chipper *clink*
of cups and teaspoons lifted from the sink.
The kettle on to boil. The radio.

She would have liked – just once – for him to say
Come on – let's go get wrecked. Or, failing that,
*Let's stay in bed. Let's stay in bed all day
and do some freaky stuff*. Or – I don't know –
Let's burn something. That fucking coffee pot
that fills and empties like a beating heart
all the livelong day – the radio,
the sink, the house, this life. *Let's burn the lot.*

It's terrible, to see him cold and clear
as what he was: full of daft ambitions,
all knife and nerve and luck and loony dreams.
It's terrible. It's terrible to think
that cups and coffee pots and kitchen sinks
were waiting, all the while, to usher them
along the dreary aisle from there to here.
I must be gone, she thinks. *I must be gone.*

I must be gone and live. Now where's that from?
She can't recall the tune, just the bassline:
da-dum da-dum da-dum da-dum da-dum.
A loosening, a sense of sweet disaster,
of every chamber breached and disarrayed;
of dancing till the dawn, of him and her
all lean and tight and quick like sparring blades –
God above. How young they were back then.

How young they were. Roll over, feel the slow
poison of the sentence sinking in.
The kettle churrs and trills. The jocund day
is shaking out its feathers, radios
are bringing news. Outside and overhead,
a happy dagger zips across the sky
and casts a whirring shadow on the bed –
but only for a second. Then it's gone.

Lore

You'll hear her, sometimes, Captain – nine fathoms down,
    and stirring in the silt. And I've heard all about her –
I've heard that pliant waist gives way to scale below the belt,

I've heard her voice is vinegar, or salt ground in a wound,
    or eight bells tolled together as you founder.
I've heard her battle ensign is a square of black and gold,
    with a little silver *kiss* for every man-o'-war she's sunk.
I've heard it's her that prickles when you're topside and alone –

    and I hear you're never topside on your own.

I heard her little jinx slunk up the gangway when we docked –
    I heard she chafed the rigging; I heard she rigged the dice.
I heard she fouled the anchor when the ship put out to sea
    and I heard she cheats at uckers when she plays.

I heard you had her inked in blue and black beneath the quay,
    I heard you licked her name around your bow;
I heard you tacked her picture in the dark above your bunk –
    and I heard the strangest sound just now – like oyster shell

    on oyster shell, or something brittle, knocking on the hull.

I've seen the piles of gutweed, folded over, piled high,
    and yes, I've heard the stories of her hair –
how a man might lose his mind there, in the green,
    trying to find the one green strand that leads him home –

    and there it is again – like razorshell

    on razorshell, or something brittle, tapping at the skull.

Click-*clink*. The nadazero. Every whirlpool, every storm,

(I'm sorry, Sir, I think we're going down)

There are no charts for this,

no following wind, and every course you plot leads back to her –
    her formal thorns, her pole, her doldrum calm,
her lucid little scrum of weed and eels, that drifts and weaves

in all the lawless currents down below. What *is* she though?
    That urchin – sharp medicine – bad star –
the marlinspike that worries at the heart and its knotted fist –

I know the mind plays games – how the ice makes flimsy pictures
    in the air above the water. But I have to wonder, Captain –
what marvellous contortion turned the girl into the monster?

Because I hear there was a time she wore your promise round her finger.
    And I hear that when she left, she left it sitting on the counter.
The dull click-*clink* of gold against formica –

how desire turns and drains in its puny hole.

Audio commentary

Here she comes. I've always loved this shot.
See how the light breaks out along her throat
in waves, as if it's spilling. *Spilling*, yes –
I said that then. Quite poignant now, I guess.

Yeah, she's a marvel here. Now hang on, Ken –
now could we just – can we see that again?
Yes, back a bit. That's right. Yes, this bit here –
she's at the table, food's already there,
she looks at him, then she looks down. Now look –
just watch her scrutinise that artichoke
as if she'd never seen the like, as if
the thing might up and bite her. That knife
remains in her left hand throughout the scene.
The artichoke, of course, will not get eaten.
That wasn't in the script. We left it in
because it's perfect. The awkwardness, I mean.
It's things like that. Those little awkward quirks.

But Jesus, Ken, it took a lot of work.
She didn't know where to look or put her feet,
we had to start from *scratch*. A lot of sweat
went into making her look effortless.
And she was young. I don't think people realise
how young she was. *Younger than her years*,
as people say. You really see it here,
I think, it takes a kind of guilelessness to make
a shot like that come off, a certain lack
of worldly scuff and wear.

Now, see that manhole there –
Yes, here we are – just look – it took us hours
to land that heel – click *clack* – upon the spot.
Fifty, sixty takes, to get that right.

Anyway, where were we Ken?
Oh yes – a nightmare for the crew. I mean,
the boys were all professionals, and she was –
well, you know.

39

Of course I feel vindicated now.
You know, I said, there's something in that girl
you won't get off the peg – a kind of *elemental
force*. A *depth of passion*. Yes, that's it.
Just watch her here – the way her eyes ignite
like burners when she speaks – that sense of *purpose* –
how all she *is* conspires to express
what she will *do* –

Well yes – haha – I've heard that story too.
I can't say if it's true or not, but then
a gentleman never tells. No, really, Ken,
enough. And that's just how she was –
quite volatile, I guess. Impetuous.
A real bag of cats. A summer storm.
And she could turn it on – that famous charm –
and turn it off as well. You never knew
from one take to the next what she would do,
so you'd get these little glints of brilliance,
like this one here – that's right – then all at once
you'd have a sulking child on your hands.
Tough job. I mean, we got there in the end,
but it was hard – for all of us – you know.
The trick, of course, was just to let her go –
to let her squall and spit and all the rest –
just get the lot, and sort it out in post.

That was how you did it. As I said –
it took a lot of work. Like trying to ride
a lightning bolt at times, like trying to hold
a bit between the teeth of something wild.
I guess that's what it was – the trick
of being what she was. A funny mix
of feral cat and sex and innocence.
If I could bottle that. The inexperience,
but also that – that sense of *withheld promise*.
She had, you know, this kind of savviness –
fox sense, as my mother used to say –
a way of being smart. Or more like *sly* –
smart with people. Smart with men, at least.

And anyway, she learned fast.
                    Just watch her getting on and off
that vaporetto like a pro, as if she'd spent her life
parading up and down the Grand Canal,
instead of waiting tables.

          Of course there's times I feel responsible.
No, no – I do, I do. You put a girl
like that in mulberry silk, and – well, you can imagine.
She's never learned restraint or discipline,
she's got no self-control –

                    Aha, now this is fun.
We cut one frame in ten, then ran it back
at double speed to get that look of shock –
No, no, that's right – the shock itself is real –
No, we didn't tell her. We wanted her to feel
as if the thing were really taking place.
You see it here – that fear upon her face.
A scene like this, it's all about the threat
of violence and how it wrings you out.
You don't get to call *cut* in real life –
that isn't how it works. It looks as if
it's real because that's what she really *felt*.

And look at the results.
                    I always said
Just look at the results. What we achieved.
A risk, of course, but worth it in the end.

          Well yes, what happened happened.

The thing is, Ken, she didn't understand
a thing about the world, or how it works.
She thought she did, of course. To hear her talk
you'd think she knew the lot. I think she thought
that being famous meant that you should get
exactly what you want. Perhaps she thought
that she'd outgrown us – she's the hot young starlet
and we were just the chumps who did the work.

You know, it's really hard for me to talk
about that time, because she didn't help herself,
she really didn't. If people knew the half
of what we had to do to keep her straight.
Because she was under contract, don't forget,
and rules are rules. I said that, *rules are rules*,
but like I said, she had no self-control,
no discipline.

And Christ Almighty, Ken, the stuff she said
towards the end –
                  But she was off her head
by then, just saying stuff, I guess,
to get attention. And you know how it is – the press –
Well, you know how it is. Just nasty stuff.
A nasty time. You wouldn't think a mouth
as sweet as that could say the things she said.
And poor old Bill – he had a wife and kids –
An awful time. Just really nasty stuff.
Hard for all of us. Well, anyway. *Enough.*

         Now hang on – can we wind that back?
Just here, the frame before we fade to black.
Just look – we got this in a single take –
her lips have parted like she's going to speak
and then – and this was Bill's idea – the sound
just drops clean out.

              You have to understand
we *knew* we had something special on our hands
if we could only make it work. The rest
is history, of course, but at the time we just
got on with it.

              Man, that final shot.

Yeah, Klaus worked bloody hard to get it right.
You know, I always said he should have had
a gong or two for that, he really should.

A beetle in a box

That's right, old friend, a beetle in a box.
The box is sealed shut and double locked:
that beetle can't get out. So let me tell you all about

Have you played the Beetle Game? Simple rules allow for the game to be played either in pairs or arranged as a Beetle Drive.

the beetle in the box.

It's blue and gold and green.
Neat and glossy, like an engine.
There's six articulated feet

As *pocket watch* won't scan.

and a sort of figure eight
which may or may not be its thorax.
It clicks and stumbles, in its box,
because it wants to come undone,
wants to split along the join,

like a locket; like a secret;
like a tacky little secret
might be hidden in a locket;

like a sneaky little poet
might say *box* but mean *a sonnet*
and then put a beetle in it.

Yes! Just the sort of stunt you might expect.
A box within a box, intrinsicate –
we'll have to do some work if we're to talk

Oh it is a world of sport to heare how some such clouting beetles rowle in their loblogicke

about that beetle. And what's worse is

I don't really have a beetle in a box.

I'm sorry, friend – no beetle, and no box.
It's a flimsy nudge-and-wink: a way to talk
about the things we talk about.

                                    Irritating, isn't it?

The street magician grinning like a twat
as he disappears your wallet, or your watch,
or that beetle we've all heard so much about.   To say nothing of the box.

§

You know, once I walked your street
from half past three to four o'clock, just to see
what it would feel like to be you.

          To replicate the way your mind lit up
when nerve and cortex met *that very* stimulus –

the cornershop; the curb; each crack and nook's
exacting combination.

          Just a glimpse would do – just one second

with all the pins and tumblers all lined up
with the *click* of working parts, articulate
and flush, precisely true.

                    And if not that, then what?

A knock-knock joke with no one at the door,   Thrust into a cupboard
no door to knock at. Four familiar walls,   among the blackbeetles
lidless, lockless, locked.

                    Best not dwell on that.

§

This afternoon, I listened as a cop described a scene –
a scene which he could see, and I could not.
The actors in the scene, in the order they appear,

They that had charge to
guyde other, were poore
blinde betels themselues.

are MAN BEHIND THE COUNTER IN THE SHOP
AROUND THE CORNER (whom I can clearly picture)
and MAN WHO STOLE MY WALLET (whom I can't).

Said theft is not depicted, but the men appear on camera –
a camera mounted just above the door
of the shop around the corner[1]

                    and this afternoon, a cop
was watching this play back upon a screen
in a backroom of his station, full of screens

for playing footage back. I've never met the cop,
or seen the private room with all the screens;

he had me on the phone, and we – the cop and I, I mean –
were trying to discuss what he could see.[2]

---

[1] The man behind the counter of the shop around the corner
handed over all his footage to the cops.
And no, I didn't care about the wallet, or the theft,

but the man behind the counter handed over
all this footage, keeps on asking if they've *cracked it*
like it's something from a thriller, keeps on asking

when I'm in for bread or milk – *Cracked it yet?*
He wants to run for councillor, and thinks
– I think he thinks – that this will help. So here we are.

[2] No, I didn't care about the wallet, or the theft,

but the cop cared even less, and all I saw were all the times
the cops had done fuck all while the woman I loved best
went down in front of us. So here we are.

45

Okay, I said. *Okay, let's try again –*

he comes and stands beside the slush machines,
he stoops, and leans his elbows on the counter.
He buys some fags, some chocolate, and some vodka.

He pays for it on card. The card is green,
or greeny-black –

             It's not easy to describe,
                     said the cop.
Dark green, perhaps?

             Perhaps. A darkish green.

A darkish green, okay –
             Or maybe black.

Okay then. From the top. Let's try again.

He sighed and pressed rewind. The cop, I mean.[3]
But think of him – that other one – the MAN
WHO'S WALKING BACKWARDS. Who doesn't want his vodka.

Who stands there, with his elbows on the counter,
as chocolate, fags and plastic bag all scatter,
and who somewhere, minutes later and off-camera,

––––––––––––––––––––

[3] He didn't join the Force to have to deal with this shit.
The guy who runs the Shop N Save, who's acting like Columbo,
and now he's got this woman on the phone

who doesn't seem to care about the wallet, or the theft,
who seems more interested in the *exact* shade of green
        or greeny-black or black her fucking card is.

will meet me up the road and slip a wallet
in my pocket.
                                     I won't see it happen.
I'll be doing up my laces, or waiting for the bus,

or thinking, as I'm thinking right this minute,
of your street, with all its cracks and nooks,
and how I traipsed along it, up and down,

and how – if I gave this to you straight –
I'm not sure that you'd hear it.
                    Okay then. From the top. Let's try again.

§

Wittgenstein said *beetle* but meant *pain*.
Now stop me if you've heard this one before,
but what I really want to tell you all about

is a rare kind of beetle I recorded
in your street, in my half an hour of footage –

how I couldn't crack the locks or see it straight
or see it like you saw it.
                              That's the one.

I don't know if you feel that. Like as not,
you're more at home with it, or just less bothered
by the formalised routine of what we mean

to one another. I suppose that must be right.
Like the exasperated cop, who said *I'm sorry
but we really can't investigate this further.*   Who also said
                                                         You're very thorough.

COMPLICATIONS

The Fly-Dressers' Guide

> It remains an extremely absorbing activity, a real mania to which
> I have become addicted, and from which I sometimes find it hard
> to tear myself away.
>
> M.C. ESCHER

The Blue Chatterer, for instance: spook-neon,
rare as radium. The lithogram cannot hope to reproduce
its brilliantine, but there are some three hundred specimens
housed at Tring, in the Museum of the Natural Sciences,

should Sir wish to see them. Think of their collector,
who marvelled that such miracles occurred *with no intelligent eye
to gaze upon their loveliness*. A collection, incidentally,
once plundered by a young man with a diamond saw

and a dazzling obsession. How close we come to mania.
The work itself, of course: the glass conservatoire
in which two supple arias are ravelled round the task.
But Sir, I know an initiate when I see one. How else to feel

the fluent kindling, the ignition; how else to know the upshot
scuffle of the will: the great detective and his rival
going at it on the Reichenbach, our little livid echo
of the Angel who rebels and falls, pinwheeling from Heaven.

How close we come to ruin. But Sir, you felt its glimmer,
coming over Cadair Idris to Tal-y-Llyn: down there,
in the night-cold, the intricate scape of cleft and structure –
the prize that clasps itself into itself. Its snapshut gem-case.

Intentional complications

Like this one here: the column tie.

Three wraps about the wrist,
then looped around,
and slipped inside, the bight
passed underneath   and all the rope

pulled tight.   The standing end

is fastened to the bed. A simple hitch
           will do the trick:

a knot should only ever be
           as complex as the work it does

     – very like a spell, in that respect.

Like any act of will.   You know,

I know a thing or two about control,
its loops and convolutions,
                    stops and holds,
that little pact

where all I know of want involves itself
with all I know about restraint –

               and yes, I wanted this.

I must have wanted this – I hid
twelve knotted bits of thread inside your house.
And every knot spelled *yes*.
And every knot – doubled over, wound around –
spelled *now*.

(A little wince –
           now, but spelled like *consequence*.)

Doubled over, wound around,
Let each one pull its little cinch   *Revolving this*
will teach you how
                              I must have wanted this.

Doubled over, wound around,
I said, as I moved through your house.
Let each one turn its little winch,
let each pull tight and fasten to
                              the wrought dark work

of consequence. The brattish riddle in the gut
that knots itself and begs to come
undone   *what's done cannot*   tell how

I ever wanted this.

                    I did. I wanted this.

            But yes, I'm frightened now
of every fluent thing my tongue could tell
if I untied it.

And where to start – And how to spell it right –
And how to move one inch

or catch your breath, when all the subtle rigging
of the plot constricts the heart –

                              I did

and didn't want this. The simplest proposition
doubles over in the knot:

its turnabout, intrinsicate
            dark world of spellbound consequence.

                    I might have said –

I might.
                    I might have said
that everything worth having, doing, making
is a knot.

There again, I might have said

that life was quite straightforward until you
snarled up the line;

and what a thing, to take on someone new
with all that mess of ribbons,
                    all ravelled round the pole

                              you know
I know a thing or two about control –

the stopstart jig of how and when to want,
when to resist,
                    when to let go,

                              you know
I know a thing or two about control
and how to lose it –

a little weed, a lot of wine,
untied my tongue enough to tell it straight –

                    that yes, I wanted this.

            I did, I wanted this, the bond

where all I know of want is stopped and held
by one taut lesson in restraint –

That you might understand. That you might not.

Hush now – tie your tongue. We mustn't tell.
We mustn't spell the name
                    or name the spell, or else

        the whole lot comes unravelled in our hands.

Giallo

The trick falls somewhere there between what you see
and what you don't. Between the cleaver coming down
and the merry spatter – another image darkens on the retina.
The mind supplies the detail that decorum must omit –
but the mind, let's not forget, has its own censors.

Now you see her, now you don't. Now watch the camera
move lovingly among the assembled treasures.
Something or other here must offer answers: the marble
or the moppet, the reddened mouth, the leather glove.
You almost had it then – a half-remembered, murmured

scrap of rhyme, a cradlesong. Like tenderness. Like trauma.
Like love, with all the notes played out of order.
Because you were rattled, weren't you, by that mirror –
by what you saw just now, or thought you saw,
reflected in the glass. The old betrayal; the awful peekaboo.

Muse

I met her once. In taffeta and ermine,
and sitting in a bar in Stepney Green.
I don't think she had slept. *Is it Monday now?*
Or Tuesday? She'd lost her purse again,

had no money. She said *Oh Honey, hey,*
you know – I used to know your man.
(She said that – said *your man*. Said *Honey, hey*.)
She talked – about herself. Said *It's funny,*

I've always been the one that got away –
I couldn't really hack the staying on,
the seeing through. Well – you know what I mean.

She smiled, so I smiled back. *Well, anyway.*
Remember me to him, won't you, Honey?
I will, I lied. And went about my day.

The true story of your own death

Afraid? Not at all. Safest form of travel.
The usual stuff, of course – superstitions,
little rituals. I'd rather sit back here, in the tail,
than up towards the nose. I always do.
I run through a scenario or two from time to time,
but everyone does that. You do it too.

I daresay there are thoughts I've thought too hard
and others I try not to think at all. Like *fuel*
paired with *combustible*. Or *metal* with *fatigue*.
And yes, I'm sure I feel the same as you
about the limits of control. That's quite normal.
Maybe once or twice – during take-off,
during landing – I've felt the barrel-roll
of real panic. But all quite quickly righted, quickly
brought within the ambit of control.
Afraid? No, not at all. No more than you.

I mean – yes – there's a tensive sort of spell
to all the little protocols involved.
The upright seats, the locked-up oxygen,
the clunking buckle. The implacable
grey bulk of thirty pounds of moulded plastic.
The armrests in position, and the bit
where someone dons the limp inflatable
and blows into a whistle –

the cheery wave towards your nearest exit.

It trips a switch, is all, shorts a circuit,
somewhere private –

It's strange, I guess. Strange to feel bored
while watching – or not watching – a rehearsal
of the worst thing that can happen.

                              And it might.

But you know what I mean –
you know you do. A kind of fascination
that cinches round disaster: around names,
and names of places. Certain numbers.
The way a name or number earns an aura
that crackles like dark static. Just listen, hear it hum

    in *empennage* and *jumpseat, aileron*;
    in *boarding, cockpit, cabin, brace, TERRAIN*.

A sort of charge that plays around precision –
the things the nerves remember when they're
bypassing the brain –

    The nine unlikely things that had to happen
    that happened all at once: how no one
    could have known about the error, the malfunction;
    how the error wouldn't matter, if procedure
    had been followed; wouldn't even matter then,
    but for one miscalculation –

    How the Captain had a dream the night before
    about falling from the sky above Miami,
    and later, told the dream to his First Officer
    who said *mm-hmm*, as he was leaning over
    to get a better look at the incomparable rear
    of the stewardess who'd just brought in their coffee –

    And the dream, and the coffee, and some comments
    on the weather, the creak and groan of plastic
    and the *mm-hmm* of the officer,
    the chatter of the instruments and all the other
    nothing-things that happen to have
    happened on that day –

    they're stuck there now, wound up in the recorder.

And think of them,
the documents – Oh God – the grim
manila-bound officialdom of Death.
Imagine it – the tedium, the reams
of printed paper. Just listen, hear it riffle

through *incident*, *event*, *default* and *mortgage*,
through *liable* and *claim* and *risk assessed* –

Rest assured, where someone else's
money is involved, your timely or untimely end
has ultimately been accounted for.

So yes, I try this airline on for size,
see how it looks in headlines, how it chimes
with a phrase like *engine failure*, *pilot error*,
or *seat numbers of survivors*. You do this too –

you know you do.

A shock, to find it here among the finite
list of things that *might just happen*, now, to *you*.
A million million ways to tell the story

but one of them is true.

But look – here come the drinks, here come
the ushers – sorry, stewards – in their suits.
Here comes the Hello Madame, Hello Sir,
Here comes the trolley with its clanking wheel.

I knew a steward once – he always said
the hardest thing to learn was how to smile.
The smile is corporate, impersonal –
it has to say two things, but those two things
don't really fit together very well.

They'll do their best to make us comfortable.
They're sorry. No exceptions to the rules.

A fine distinction

The instinct for self-preservation is matched, in variable
proportions, by the instinct for destruction.

ALBERT CAMUS, 'Reflections on the Guillotine'

She likes the cut
of this one's jib,

likes its clean
no-nonsense schtick –

the stern rebuke, but thus finessed.

There is in her,
she knows, this streak
that begs for discipline.

She pictures it, from time to time,

her head in the lunette. No
fuss now. Come,

but make it quick –

un souffle frais sur la nuque

Oh, little duke. Such etiquette.

All the blues

If you were told 'There is a ghost in the next room',
and believed it, you would feel, indeed, what is often
called fear, though of a different kind.

C.S. LEWIS

But how many here in the house?

One in the scullery,
one in the flue,
one in the intricate hush of the blue jacaranda.

Lift up the lid and count all the blues

icarus, bellargus, corridon, chalk

One like a gas flame   one like a spark
one like the lift of the light in the blue jacaranda.

Fly away Peter

Fly away Paul

how many over and under the fibres
of linen and coverlet, *mother, forget me not,*

vinca and gentian, scilla, delphinium

One like a pilot and one like a light
and one saying something like
something like blue jacaranda.

Say you woke in the night   in a hospital bed
and threw out your arms   but your darlings were dead

and now
there's these strangers instead.

These lily-white figures in slick alabaster,
their milk and their porcelain bells, and the click

of their instrument chatter

you'll never you'll never

You never will grow it in England. Not blue jacaranda.

Come beetle   come knocking
                        a mouse in the skirting

is clutching its parcel of bones   ear turning inwards
to hammer and incus   the tick

                    of the blood running slow

then something like starlight and something like swifts
and an uprush of blue and then black and then nothing.

Rune poem for a funeral

The charm, being an integrated unit, is only capable of success if it is read or
chanted in its entirety. Runes rely for their effect, at least as far as we can tell,
on the mystery attached to each individual symbol.

JOHN MCGREGOR, *An Edition of the Old English Metrical Charms*

Today, I will be borrowing the runes.
I will be borrowing the runes as little sticks
to wind the day around. I find,
or I have found,
that any formal frame will do the trick;
and as it happens, I've just read a book

on Anglo-Saxon runes and metric charms,
where little glowing strokes
do this and that, stand in for things,
do bindings, banishings.
Something to confer a little order –
better that, than take the day served neat.

Odin did this once. He fought a snake
or else a grief – I can't remember which –
went after it with *glory-sticks*
or *wuldortanas* – nine of them – and each
was supercharged. *These nine,*
the poem goes, *have strength against nine poisons* –

and no, I'm not a god, I never hung
nine windswept nights upon a sacred tree.
Never *howling took them up* nor *fell back down*.
But listen, pal, I'll take
whatever gets me through today,
so unless you've got diazepam, it's runes.

Yew tree: forlorn sentinel. Coy
hullaballoo of collared doves.
Faith and its folded wings.

The grave. The overburdened
fact of it: the way it opens under
every gesture, thought or act.

The day. And how the past
is bounded by it, running
fast and cold within its cut.

The Little Brook. In Basingstoke.
Dear God, I never thought
it would be Basingstoke.

There is no little brook,
so why's it called *The Little Brook.*
While we're at it, why's it called a *wake.*

Can't remember. Useless glyph
I'm treading round the car park,
smoking cigarettes I didn't want.

Egg sandwiches, reliable
as Death itself, and which I am,
for no good reason, stuffing in my

mouth, while from my

mouth spills stupid stuff, like

yes, we had the weather, no,
you'll want to take the M11,
yes, a lovely service, yes yes yes

Some remarks on the General Theory of Relativity

Space, it turns out, curves.
                    Space itself.
            And time does too, or rather
space and time together curve and stretch
wherever there is matter. And this has always been the case,

but no one thought to tell me. Practically, this means
that if I lived up a mountain,
and my twin lived by the sea, then one or other of us
                would be younger than the other.

            I don't have a twin. I've got an older brother
who says we never landed on the moon.
An uncle, who thinks aliens are farming us as food,
who says The End Is Coming
                        and Coming Very Soon.
An aunt who liked cocaine – who had the Seven Sisters
tattooed across her back when she got clean.
And a father, who took off like a comet when he could,
who won't be coming back this way again,
not in this life.

                As for me,
            my sense of things in general
is loosely sentimental. And outer space, with all its baudequin
            of quark and antiquark and light and dark
is no exception. I like the bits that look like us, that look

like human things.
                A little spooky action.
Some unexpected pairing, locked in formal equilibrium.
I like the null and void of a black hole, but only
            – let's be honest – as a vehicle
where the tenor is depression.
Beyond that, I find I'm fairly chilled
by distances and zeros, by emptiness and lack,
                by the eerie little whine in the word *vacuum*.

Last night, washing dishes, I looked up to see my neighbour
staring at her sink, with all her dishes
piled beside her –
                    a mirror-trick, configured
by the way the houses here have of bending round each other.

Our paths don't ever cross – we keep our different hours –
but the houses here are small, the walls are thin.
I hear her talking, sometimes, on the phone,
I hear her cough at night. I hear the little *clunk*
of the cabinet in her bathroom –

        the same cheap bathroom cabinet
that I have in my bathroom –
the same cheap clunking cabinet all landlords put in flats.
                    And yes, I must assume

she hears that little *clunk*. She hears me cough at night.
She hears me talking, sometimes, on the phone,
she's thought *These walls are thin.*
She's looked up from her sink to see her twin
in a square of yellow kitchen-light, with ten dark feet between.

– then the knife-edge found my finger, and it came up
red and sudden –
                    that scandalous reminder
of all that ties us down and ropes us off from one another.

Ghost story in the subjunctive

Suppose you woke thinking – as I did today –
of couplings and joins in our bodies.
Hinges and pivots   folded and sprung   in the heap of our resting bodies.

Suppose that you didn't. Suppose it's the one
that's clinkered with all of the others.
Mortis and tenon   Bone onto bone   Angles of lift and rotation.

Suppose there's a catch – some sort of pin –
that holds us to these soft bodies.
Testing the weight of the thought of it gone by watching your sleeping body.

Say it were dawn. Distal and grey
on the very last day of December.
The fingerbone day. The tap on the shoulder, says *One of these days is the one.*

Already too late.
                        It was always too late.
Already too late to have been with your body
when it was the body you knew.
              Too late to be able to hear what they sing

when you're strapped to the mast and they're singing for you.
And the past got there first and the past did its work
and it sunk all its swivels and hooks into you.

                        You're done, you're run through.

White breath on the glass – *last gasp* – or a toast
to our tenuous guests –

fog on the mirror   or smoke in the parlour
  and Lord they get lively when everything's vapour

A host of them here, in the grey of the room,
growing bolder and solid and shrill and full-bodied –

that you never wake   that you wake alone
  that this was the dream   that we wake somewhere else
that you lie with her   that I leave you, alone

and asleep at your post.
                    Last chance. *Almost.*

Love, what is done is as blunt as a bone
and all out in front is just wishes and breath –

  Except for that one thing. Except for that one.

And I know it I know it I know it I know

when that gibbering ghoul starts up his old tune –
you are bones   you are bones   you are hung
on a trellis of bones. You are hinged on this spine

and the old year swings out and around on its pivot
and you will be leaving – or I will – and soon
and as sure and as quick as the breath leaves the body.

Oversight

Rilke had Angels, had
Junctions of light, corridors, stairs, thrones,

but look what we've got: the blue afternoon
and the pavement. A pineapple soda.
A hangover fit for two sinners

                  and man, did we earn it.

Come on, let's go.
Let's bother that seraph
            who's curled like a wretch
on the stucco outside of the Kingdom.
All bed hair and one beamish buttock, a wing
pulled over his head like a coverlet.

            Not now, he says. *Maybe later.*

Let's run along down to the cemetery then,
let's read all the stones.
               Let us pray

that Heaven will spare us the sudden,
the solitary mirror. I know that you've seen it,
old friend, and let's face it,
            the news is unkinder each day.

          So let us be thankful. Let's say

that if we must do this, if we must rehearse
our senescence by feeling like death
every weekend, for God's sake let's do it together.

THE SQUINT

All interesting facts are presented as briefly as possible.

A. NEEDHAM, *How to Study an Old Church*

I

In the chancel is a narrow, low window, called to this day 'the Lepers' window', through which, it is concluded, the lepers who knelt outside the building witnessed the elevation of the host at the altar.

Notes and Queries, No.37

What's it like? A little like a cut,
although it *is* a cut. Ditto apertures of different kinds
(eyelet, coin-slot, arrow slit).
Too trim to be an inkblot. Nothing to see inside

except a strip of dark I recognise
with the crackshot, eyeless knowing of the nerves.

We stood there for a minute, looking in.
I thought some thoughts. I tied a knot or two
between this thought and that. You must have done the same –

this is, you understand, a partial view.

II

I looked into the cut – and you did too –
but I'll go first. I'll start with what I know.

I know this dark. Silence has a pitch
and I know this one well, know all the low
vibrations in its key. The seasoned oak,
the balusters, the fluent scrolls and reels.
Lilies. Opened throats. Oasis. Smoke.
A painted heart, with thorns. A resting bell.

The borders of the shape. Its halt and hold,
its havening insistence: *Stop right there.*
The firm hand, the answering pressure.
The closest thing I know to bliss, this
sweet relief of measure, sweet release
of being told: *There now. That's enough.*

You, of course. I'd know you anywhere
by the nimble little streak of heat or luck
that prints itself like lightning on the air
whenever you are here, and all around you.
I know it, but I don't know what to call it.
Your signature. Your rune. Your afterglow.

III

Half thoughts, dashed off in shorthand
in no particular order –

Skin. As semi-porous. Skin
                as barrier. As border.
I bore about with me
                an inward wound.
My reaching hand,
           that reached about for yours
                (touched your side)

Welcome
        on the bridge across the border.

  And if I
      if I said
            My reaching hand
My reaching hand, that reached
and thrust my hand into his side.

And if I said
            And would you understand
welcome   crossing
  come   across   a border

and where I end   and where
                and where you end
                   and when

                 and when

Our bodies, all dressed up before the altar.

IV

Corbel, chancel, apse. We know the names
but not where they belong. We lift the lid
on each one like a music box instead, and feel the notes
turn back to stone and brass and polished wood.

I didn't know you then. And when we strayed,
we strayed our separate ways. Nonetheless,
there are lines we could recite in unison
and spells that bound us then that bind us still

and that's a kind of knowing, I suppose –
a way to be where you are. Or where you were.
*Chill tall draught of chapel air. Brusque
hello of braided wool.* You in your pitchpine pew,

three hundred miles and thirteen years from where
I sit in mine, intoning the same prayer.
Even the word itself – its aperture. We hear it now
and bow our heads like sheepish truants do.

V

A way to be where you are. That's the trick.
Call it an excursion – a little exercise
in sympathetic occupation.

                             Goes like this –

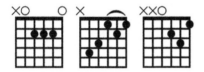

The same three chords, played round and round and round
the way we liked them played, when we were –

                      You know. You remember.

We partied, drank, got laid,
                      and all the while,

the same three chords went round and round, and now
we're stuck this way. Besotted. Hopeless. Hooked.

                    You there, in the corner.

You there, listening
to the same three chords that I did

                You. Yes, you there. Listening

to the same three chords that I did, getting wound around
the same cheap thrills. Stuck and spelled like me, so that
A, C#, Dm
can scratch out twenty years and land its needles somewhere tender.

                    Yes. I have you now.

My heart – it isn't clever.
Roll the perforated foil, it goes like a pianola.
And yours is just the same.
it goes A, C#, Dm,

                    Why don't you shut the door

VI

A way to be where you are. That's the spell,

                  except the scene

is somehow sullen. The colours all turned down,
the air a little stale.
Underneath, a trace of something final –

        like vinyl in the attic, or like landfill.

Something to do with how the thing's sustained
on three cheap chords, played round and round, and how

the same three chords, played round and round and round
can rig this sneaky trespass, but can't
keep the future off

       (and the future's got its goons, and they play *rough*).

Something to do with that. Or just the trick
of knowing things you don't. To see the harm
that's coming to you coming up the stair. To have to hear
the key change throw its cloud across the sun,

               I couldn't stop it now. No one can.

VII

Let's have a name for that.
Not harm, but what comes after:
the formal aftermath of damage done.

It's hard to hit that note. I know the ones
that bleed or blurt, demanding
quick attention – little tender words,

and good alarms for urgent problems.
(The scar is hot, the wound is wet.
Their scandals are still young.)

The formal aftermath of damage done
is the derangement of a structure
and – for this and other reasons –

I would choose the term *a grief*.
I like its stoniness, its gritted teeth,
the fact it won't be fixed, the way it speaks

to what was *suffered* or *sustained*.
I like its bevelled edge, its slenderness.
It is a kind of opening – and if

what opened it no longer causes pain,
then that's as well; I'd only cavil
that it's different, on the outside looking in.

VIII

I know that what I saw was incomplete –

(It's maddening, to have this stuff inside
and have it stall, halfway to being said.)

I know that what I saw was incomplete,
but that was only part of what I knew,
and that was less again than what I thought,
and that was less than what I understood.

A bit like that – a bit less awkward though.
You know the trick: the arrow leaves the bow,
the runner seems to run upon the spot.
That one, yes. But something isn't right
in the way things subdivide and subdivide,

the way the runner falters and recedes
and logic and proportion drop down dead.
It's hard, you know, saying something straight
with half a chance of being understood.
It's hard. It's even harder to be intimate
when my best runner can't get out the gate.

IX

In the car on the way back home, I let an old cassette
sing *I feel better, I feel better,*

                and what had got to me
– though I don't think I can say this very clearly –
what had got to me was all that time before we met.

Tell me something, tell me something. Over and over.
The sentimental clarity of detail –
what happened, how and why, and when and where,
and every grief you took. That most of all.

There's no unknowing it. And what a tough instruction,
when it goes on kicking out the same dumb pain
it always will.
             But if I don't see that, then what
exactly am I looking at. Old horror of the inkblot,
of the dark, of the mirror – of finding that you really are alone.

X

Later, I pulled off one glove, and stared
at the skin beneath, and then – to my surprise –
brought it to my face and held it there.

I couldn't tell you if that's true or not.
I mean, it might as well be true, because
it sounds as if it's true. But if you want it plainer,
then might as well say

                 Look, I am more scared
than I let on, but also full of love
                       sometimes joy
and mostly just unsure of what to do

and look, I do believe in grief, and grief
as aperture, and aperture

as how we see ourselves   *see each other*
                       and it's late

        and getting later. There's that too.

SPARKS

The empty hotel corridor was dark.
But here the keyhole shone, a meaning spark.

THOM GUNN, 'The Corridor'

As many of the poems here feature titles that run straight into the poem, they leave no room for an epigraph; nonetheless, many were sparked by a borrowed line or phrase. These notes offer all the orphaned sparks that never made it onto the page, together with acknowledgements for bits and bobs borrowed from here and there.

The brain of the rat in stereotaxic space (11)

The title tweaks *The Rat Brain in Stereotaxic Coordinates*, by George Paxinos and Charles Watson.

In the dream of the cold restaurant (16)

Lines 21 and 22 are taken from A.A. Brill's translation of *The Interpretation of Dreams*.

COVERS (29)

To intimate is to communicate with the sparest of signs and gestures, and at its root intimacy has the quality of eloquence and brevity. But intimacy also involves an aspiration for a narrative about something shared, a story about both oneself and others that will turn out in a particular way.

Lauren Berlant, *Intimacy*

Would someone with a hard face please protect me from those sickly and sugared old tunes? They tinkle-tinkle their simple sweetness and yet somehow complicated accusations out of the most personally demeaning residues of what had seemed to be lost and gone forever.

Dennis Potter, *The James MacTaggart Memorial Lecture*

I Think We're Alone Now (31)

The italicised spindle around which the poem is wound is taken from the 1967 hit 'I Think We're Alone Now', written by Ritchie Cordell and recorded by Tommy James and the Shondells.

Whatever happened to Rosemarie? (34)

The title is taken from the 1963 Connie Francis song of the same name.

A beetle in a box (43)

> Solidarity is not discovered by reflection but created. [...]
> The process of coming to see other human beings as 'one of us' rather than as 'them' is a matter of detailed description of what unfamiliar people are like and of redescription of what we ourselves are like.
>
> Richard Rorty, *Contingency, Irony, and Solidarity*

The marginal glosses are all taken from the OED's exemplary quotations under the entry for *beetle*.

COMPLICATIONS (49)

> A knot is never 'nearly right'; it is either exactly right or it is hopelessly wrong.
>
> Clifford Ashley, *The Ashley Book of Knots*

The Fly-Dressers' Guide (51)

The epigraph is taken from Escher's *The Regular Division of the Plane*.

Intentional Complications (52)

> that dark land of consequences
> promised by Ariadne
>
> Stephen Dobyns, 'Theseus Within the Labyrinth'

Giallo (55)

For *giallo* enthusiasts: the film that prompted the poem was Argento's *Profondo Rosso*.

The true story of your own death (57)

The title translates a phrase from Borges' 'The Library of Babel': *la relación verídica de tu muerte*. The poem itself was prompted by a line spoken by Denholm Elliott in the film *The Night My Number Came Up*:

> 'You realise that every detail has come true, and that only one remains, and that that one will come true, sure as fate, unless you stop it now.'

All the blues (62)

The epigraph is taken from Lewis's *The Problem of Pain*.

Oversight (70)

The line of Rilke is taken from A.S. Kline's translation of the *Duino Elegies*.

There's a pub in London called *Paradise by way of Kensal Green*, and on the wall of the pub is a figure that may or may not be an angel. He looks like he hasn't got out of bed yet, like maybe he won't be getting up till this afternoon, like he's not getting up till someone brings him a bacon sandwich. A very old friend of mine lives nearby, so I only ever see this maybe-angel when I'm hungover.

The name of the pub is taken from the final lines of Chesterton's 'The Rolling English Road':

> And see undrugged in evening light the decent inn of death;
> For there is good news yet to hear and fine things to be seen,
> Before we go to Paradise by way of Kensal Green.

The Squint (73)

The line *I bore about with me an inward wound* is on loan from Nennius' *History of the Britons.* The italicised lines at the base of pages 77 and 78 are borrowed from Pulp's 1995 album track 'Underwear', and those on page 81 are from Radiohead's 1993 track 'Lurgee'.

MIX
Paper from
responsible sources
FSC® C007785
www.fsc.org

Printed in the USA
CPSIA information can be obtained
at www.ICGtesting.com
JSHW082117060524
62631JS00002B/13